Israel
by
Erwin Fieger

Israel
by
Erwin Fieger

Accidentia Druck- und Verlags-GmbH

2nd edition 1977 by
Accidentia
Druck- und Verlags-GmbH,
Düsseldorf, Graf-Adolf-Str. 112

1977 for the photographs
for all countries in the
International Copyright
Union by Erwin Fieger

Text: Hermann Lewy

Translation:
Susan Salms-Moss,
Jerry Marchand (F.i.T.)

Offset reproductions in
four colors in the format of
24 x 36 mm: Helmut Peter
Conrad KG, Solingen-Wald

Production: J. Fink Druckerei,
Ostfildern 4/Stuttgart

Conception and design:
Erwin Fieger

ISBN: 3-920005-04-X
Printed in West Germany

Hermann Lewy

Firmly rooted in the hearts and minds of the Jews of the world is a belief in Israel, in the land that belonged to their forefathers. Never has the hope vanished from their minds that the day would come when they would again live in the land promised by God. This love of the land is expressed in many varied ways. Since the day their own land was destroyed and their forefathers were thrown into exile, their fervent desire has never weakened to be brought, even after death, to their final resting place in the Holy Land. Observant Jews in the Diaspora have a handful of sand from the Promised Land strewn on their graves, so that, at least symbolically, their longing might be fulfilled to finally rest in the earth of Israel.

"Israel," so reads an ancient saying, "is the center of the world, and Jerusalem is the center of that land." For one who does not adhere to the Jewish religion or who sees in it nothing but a nebulous mysticism, the point of view expressed by this quotation may seem naive, arrogant, and incompatible with modern forms of society. For Jews, however, this saying plays a central role. It has become the heart of their religious and day-to-day life. The fate of the city of Jerusalem and of the land of Israel links the members of Judaism in a mysterious way, even though the majority of them do not live there, indeed, know neither the city nor the country. This belief originates, to a large extent, in the Biblical promise made to Abraham: "And I give to you and your seed this land" – this Israel!

God's promise is repeated often in the Old Testament. It guides the Jew's thinking and determines, as history up to the present time has shown us, his goals. No other religion is so closely tied to the never-diminishing longing for Zion, with the possible exception of the crusaders and the pilgrims of other monotheistic beliefs who made pilgrimages to Zion.

Efforts to explain the two contradictory elements which seem to be inherent in this longing have never ceased. On the one side – it is said – Judaism claims that its religious values, its ethics, are universal and that, as it has been foretold, the time will come when peace and justice will rule the earth, when God's kingdom will be established and all children of the earth will sanctify the name of the one God. On the other hand, just plain separatism is emitted by this longing, as Jews have at all times maintained the Zionist striving to make the Holy Land become a reality as a Jewish State. This purpose is unbending, although they have been forced to live a much longer time in exile than they have actually lived independently in that land.

This dream has also found expression in day-to-day Jewish life. The devout Jew, whenever he joins with others of the same confession to worship, turns toward Jerusalem. No synagogue, no Jewish place of worship on the five continents violates this custom. Does not the religious Jew, who prays three times a day at home, also turn his body in this direction? In the same sense, in the benedictions that are part of the marriage ceremony, the words are repeated, "Soon, oh Eternal One, may the voices of joy and wonder again be heard in the cities of Judea and in the streets of Jerusalem." And, in the same tone, the rabbi speaks to the mourners at the grave of their dear one, "May the Omnipresent comfort you among the others that mourn for Zion and Jerusalem." When the most solemn Jewish holiday, the Day of Atonement, Yom Kippur, comes to an end, the worshipper prays to the creator of this earth, his only God, "Bring us, Almighty One, to Zion." And he reminds us fervently on this day, as well as at the end of the Passover Seder, of the successful exodus of the Children of Israel from Egypt: "L'shana hab'ba'a v'Yerushalayim!" – Next year in Jerusalem! – It was King

David who chose Jerusalem as the capital city of his land.

The three monotheistic confessions cling to the sacredness of this city. For Christianity, the Church of the Holy Sepulchre is the center point of the religion. For Mohammedans, Jerusalem occupies, after Mecca and Medina, the position of the third holy site; nevertheless, the most sacred shrine of Islam is the Al Aqsa Mosque. These centers of worship have been more or less maintained throughout all the chaos of the centuries. The holiest site for Judaism is a ruin, namely, the small portion of the wall on the Temple Hill which has remained intact since the destruction of the Second Temple by the Romans. This relic of the Temple of Herod has become a center for the Jews' lamentations over the desolation in the year 70, and at the same time for mourning over Israel's long exile. In the era of automation and nuclear weapons, the Wailing Wall has remained, as always, a place – although not always an accessible one – for prayers and supplications. Many an Israeli or world traveler has written his wish down and placed the piece of paper in a niche in the Wall, in the inextinguishable hope or naive conviction that the wish will come true. A prayer here is a profession of thoughts of Israel's early splendor and of the hope in the reconstruction.

Today, the new city of Jerusalem is the seat of the Israeli President, of the Knesset (the Israeli Parliament), of the Government, of the Supreme Court. Also within its walls are the Hebrew University, the Israel Museum, as well as many buildings involved in the scientific, social, and cultural life of the Jewish State. The numerous synagogues, monumental buildings mixed with hardly-noticeable prayer rooms, are proof that a significant portion of the population continues to lead a religious life in its way. But today, as earlier, efforts are being made to shift away from a literal interpretation of the religious laws – which can be exemplified by daily life in the orthodox section, Mea She'arim – toward progressive, liberal Judaism.

The youth of Israel is familiar with the Bible and with religious history, as they are the object of study in school. Many Israelis – and not only the young ones – consider themselves non-religious, which, however, in no way means that they reject the religious tradition, the responsibilities of Judaism, and the feeling of belonging to the Jewish people, to its common fate. In fact, a noticeable characteristic of Israeli society is just this co-existence of many varied Jewish-religious and non-religious ways of life.

The position of the Church, here, of course, the Synagogue, in Israel differs greatly from that in other western countries; but, to a great extent, it fits the conditions of the country, its history, and its population. The Church is not separated from the State; yet religion has not been raised to the position of state religion on the basis of a formally written or constitutional law, which would grant certain privileges to members of that religion, while members of other religious groups would have to accept disadvantages. The present system is a middle path: it obliges the government to maintain a sympathetic attitude toward all religious groups, without intervening in their affairs.

Disagreements about the use of religious laws and principles occasionally affect public life. These may involve problems of religious education, keeping of the Sabbath, and laws involved with running the household (Kashrut). Discussions have also arisen over a question which, because of immigration and publication of statistics, is always current: Who is a Jew? That is, how can Jewish nationality (le'om) be defined? In 1958, this debate led to a cabinet crisis, which flared up again in 1970, when a majority of the Supreme Court gave a Jewish father, married to a non-Jewish woman, permission to register his children as "Jewish by nationality." The Knesset, however, passed a law saying that only those individuals born to a Jewess or to a woman converted to Judaism could be recognized as Jewish and registered as "Jewish by nationality." In the middle of 1970, the controversy broke out again over conversions to Judaism performed by reformed rabbis or others not recognized by the Chief Rabbinate.

The five books of the Pentateuch (Bible) are the sources one must dip into in order to gather significant information about the first thousand years of the history of the people of Israel. It is estimated that the first books stem from the 7th century before Christ; some portions may be even older. Their creation was later placed at about the 14th and 13th centuries before Christ; it is especially remarkable, if one looks back, given the limited development in the skills and possibilities of man at that time, that he was able to produce such writings.

The patriarchs Abraham, Isaac, and Jacob, who are members of the Jewish people, are at the same time patriarchs of Christianity. In Catholic prayers, their names appear 67 times; Protestants and Mohammedans also mention their names in prayers. Despite the fact that Jesus of Nazareth was born Jewish, Catholics and Protestants have pursued the Jews and marked them as a nation of deists. Shortly before his death on June 5th, 1973, Pope John XXIII, a trailblazer of Catholicism toward restitution after two thousand years of inflicted injustice, drew up a supplication which in part read: "We recognize that blindness has covered our eyes for many, many centuries, so that we could no longer see the beauty of Thy chosen people and no longer recognized in its face the features of our first-born Brother. We acknowledge that the mark of Cain is upon our brow. For centuries Abel lay ill in blood and tears, because we forgot Thy love. Forgive us for the curse that we unjustly spoke against the name of the Jews. Forgive us for having crucified Thee again for the second time in their flesh. For we did not know what we did . . ." This honest confession by the prelate of the Church speaks for itself.

The family of Abraham and his descendents consisted of a tribe of nomadic shepherds which moved out of

Mesopotamia, present-day Iraq, into the land of Israel. For the first time in the history of mankind, they believed in a single God, rejecting polytheism. Later, God gave Jacob the name Israel for this land, and Jacob's twelve sons, fathers of the twelve tribes, were together called the Children of Israel. The tomb of the fathers of the tribes, the Cave of Machpelah in Hebron, has been holy up to our present era, for Jews as well as for Mohammedans. Parts of the construction are more than 2000 years old; they are also mentioned by other nonbiblical sources.

Today the State of Israel looks after this and other sites and encourages archeological excavations.

Later, the Children of Israel wandered into Egypt. For the first time, it was not the restlessness of the Jewish nomads which drove them from place to place or the search for feed for their herds of cattle, still within the boundaries of their own country. For the first time, adverse circumstances – which have almost incessantly befallen them throughout the course of their history in a struggle for naked survival – forced them into involuntary exile. This time it was hunger which forced them to forsake the land and move on to Egypt. However, that country did not bring the fulfillment of their wishes and dreams to the Jewish people; instead they were used for hard labor.

Under the leadership of their deliverer, Moses, who is considered the most significant prophet and leader of Jewish history, they reached the Promised Land – although only after his death and after forty years, in which generations came and went, after wanderings of untold difficulties, during which God made a covenant with them, as they accepted the Ten Commandments. Through Moses' guidance, a group of disjointed tribes, which had somehow scraped along through centuries as an oppressed and splintered minority, had joined and found a national goal. Moses is the law-giver of monotheism, which he united with a system of social, juridical, and religious regulations. It was he who fully transformed the life and faith of his people. The radiance of his personality has determined a considerable part of Jewish civilization up to today.

The 13th to the 11th centuries before Christ witnessed the conquest of Israel by the twelve tribes under the leadership of Joshua. The people settled on both sides of the Jordan. For about two centuries, tribal autonomy existed, a period that is known as the Period of the Judges, because the leaders of the tribes considered the administration of justice to be their central duty.

After the death of the first king, Saul, his successor, David, and his son, Solomon, called Solomon the Wise, the realm was divided into two parts: Judea, with Jerusalem as its capital, which was ruled by several dynasties over the years. This was the era of incessant fighting for the belief in a single God against the widespread idolatry, which had already shown its rudiments in the dance around the golden calf in the time of Moses.

Israel's independence was brought to an end by the Assyrian conquest of 722 B.C. What happened? A part of the population was sentenced to exile. The descendents of those that survived in the Kingdom of Israel, the Samaritans, today exist as a small ethnic and religious group in Nablus and in Israel. However – this should be remarked in passing – they do not celebrate the two national Jewish holidays, Purim and Chanukah, because they are not mentioned in the Pentateuch, to which they adhere.

In the year 586 B.C.E., the Babylonians conquered

Judea. They destroyed the First Temple and deported a large number of the inhabitants to Babylon, today's Iraq. A small number succeeded in fleeing. Their goal was Egypt, where, from that time on, a numerically strong Jewish community grew, as it did in Iraq where, at the time, some families chose to remain behind. They became blossoming communities, in the religious as well as the cultural aspects. Today there are only about 500 Jews living in Egypt, whereas in Iraq one can no longer speak of a Jewish existence at all. But at that time it was here that the spark began which cultivated faith in the return to Zion and the reconstruction of a national existence.

The words of the prophets can be found in the Bible. Their words became more than words; they were lived by and served as the message for the fight for social justice. – Let us now briefly recall a few more events:

In about the 5th century B.C., the Jews were able to return to their land for the second time, as the Babylonian Empire had been overthrown by the Persians. King Cyrus of Persia allowed the Jews to return. It was to his credit that the reconstruction of the Temple was permitted. Later the suzerainty of the Persians fell to that of the Greeks; Hellenic thought clashed with Jewish thought.

In 168 B.C., the Hellenistic ruler of Syria, Antiochus Epiphanes IV, attempted to restrict Jewish autonomy and to replace the monotheistic belief by polytheism. The differences between the regime and the oppressed Jews found release in an uprising by the Hasmoneans. Victory was on the side of the original inhabitants; they won back their complete independence. The Kingdom of Judea was from then on ruled by the Hasmoneans and later by Herod. Under his rule, mighty buildings were constructed, among which the most impressive was the new Temple. The Wailing Wall and archeological excavations which have been carried out recently in the vicinity show the extent of construction under Herod. For a long period of time, Jerusalem became an important metropolis with 200,000 inhabitants, which was at that time an unbelievably large population.

The sphere of influence of the Roman Empire, encroaching upon the land, kept expanding, beginning in the year 63 B.C. After the death of Herod, the Romans intensified their barbaric methods of rule, curbing all

opposition by their might
and power. That year marks
the birth of Jesus of Nazareth.

The Roman might, jurisdiction
without rights, arbitrary
oppression, the Caesarian
period with all its negative
aspects, the origins of a new
monotheistic religion,
Christianity, all brought on
The Jewish War, which
reached its climax in the year
70 with the destruction of
Jerusalem and the Second
Temple. Three years later,
Masada, the last fortress of
Jewish resistance, which has
gone down in history in
the form of an epic poem,
was conquered by the
Romans.

During this period, the

Jewish religion brought the social and legal system it had created to a still higher level in its development. The confrontation of the Jewish culture with the Hellenistic and the Roman led to a conflict over the preservation of the Jewish character, to a fight over the retention of the Jewish tradition and its precepts of the time. Judaism has survived this struggle, although the influence of both foreign cultures can still be detected.
the Mamelukes, the Ottoman The Roman oppressors were followed by the Byzantines, the Arabs, the Crusaders,

Turks, and, before the proclamation of the third state of the Jews, the English.

These foreign rulers – with the exception of the crusaders, who came out of Central Europe in several waves – governed it no differently than if it had been a province of their empires. The crusaders established an independent realm; but they were a small, foreign caste and never grew into a nation.

The British had received the League of Nations Mandate over the country which they in turn – after other rulers had given the land, as well as Jerusalem, other names – named Palestine. Originally the British Mandate over Palestine extended to both sides of the Jordan. In 1922, however, Great Britain divided the Mandate area into Palestine, west of the Jordan, and Trans-Jordan, east of the Jordan. The total population, which was once supposed to have amounted to 3 million Jews, had shrunk to a total of 250,000.

At the granting of the Mandate, Arab resistance broke out. Bloody terrorism against the Jewish settlements was mustered in the land. The armed Arab uprising continued until 1939, the attacks on Jews and their dwellings never ceasing. To a great barbaric extent, this Arab terrorism continues even today.

England capitulated to them.

The British government under Neville Chamberlain enacted the White Book of May 17, 1939. It decreed that during the next five years only 15,000 more Jews would be permitted to immigrate to Palestine, and it contained the declaration that it was not England's goal to make Palestine into a nation, even though Lord Arthur James Balfour, the British Foreign Minister, had, on November 2nd, 1917, through Lord Lionel Walter Rothschild, made the famous Declaration to the Zionist movement, which read: "His Majesty's government regards with favour the establishment of a national homeland for the Jewish people in Palestine."

In the hour of the most menacing danger for European Judaism, the rescuing gate had been slammed shut, save for a tiny crack! Churchill considered himself called upon to lash out at the White Book in the House of Commons as the "breach of a solemn obligation," as a "new Munich." The idea of Zionism had landes in the works of world politics, in which the fate of the individual doesn't count.

In desperation, thousands of refugees, on their way to Palestine by sea, attempted to land. They had fled from their native countries under cover of night, in a desperate attempt to escape the Nazi sword of Damocles

which hung over their lives.
They had only one goal,
Palestine, the land of their
forefathers. Jewish assistance
agencies, thanks to the
generosity of Jews, particularly of the Americans, who
were able, in time of need,
to come up with sums
going into the millions of
dollars, reached out rescuing
hands. But often they were
put asea by unscrupulous
captains in jam-packed
ships, hardly seaworthy,
called, with Jewish irony,
"coffin ships." Most of them
were stopped by the British
fleet. The "illegal" immigrants
could save themselves from
the gas chambers, it was
true, but their fate was to be
locked up in detention
camps on foreign islands,

on Cyprus and Mauritania. Still, some European refugees succeeded, with the help of organizations in Palestine, when night had fallen over the coast, in treading onto the shore of Palestine – their new-old homeland.

The world knew of the thwarted rescue attempts. It was well informed about the disastrous results of the British immigration policy, which almost amounted to a complete block of immigration. England then added the final touch to all of this: an application for the immigration of 20,000 Polish children was turned down. This amounted to a death sentence!
In 1940, the "Patria" explod-

ed in the Port of Haifa. 259 people were killed! In 1941, the "Struma", coming from Romania with 768 refugees, sank in a storm off Istanbul. One single survivor! These are a few – scanty – facts out of the sad chapter written by the British Mandate. Behind dry figures stand thousands and thousands of individual fates, a sea of suffering and tears – and deaths.

130,000 Jews volunteered to be taken into the British army, which was operating in the North African Theater after the outbreak of the Second World War and which initially had serious difficulties warding off and defeating the German troops. The English hesitated. Were they afraid that, among these volunteers from that national-socialist hell, there were collaborators of the Nazi Fifth Column? Since times were tough, the British took the 30,000 Jewish fighters into their ranks anyway. "We are fighting the war on England's side as if there were no White Book," declared David Ben-Gurion, "and we are fighting against the White Book as if there were no war!" Only as of 1944 was Jewish Palestine permitted to participate in battles against the Axis Powers. Under the blue-and-white flag, the Jewish brigade went to the front. It was active in the Italian campaign and participated in the liberation of Germany from the Nazi yoke. As the war came to an end, it became apparent, even for those who had not recognized it earlier, that British policy would continue to oppose the establishment of a Jewish national homeland in Palestine and the extensive immigration of Jewish refugees. The Jewish community did not wait to answer. It began a direct fight against the British colonial power in Palestine. In this struggle there were two major goals: to force the British to relinquish the Mandate and to enable the refugees to enter the country. Resistance organizations were formed. These were the Haganah, which followed the instructions of the official Jewish channels in Palestine, and the underground organizations. While the official Jewish authorities continued to promote Ha'apalah, the illegal immigration, the Irgun Tswai'i Le'umi, an underground movement, came forth with violent measures, conducting guerilla warfare against the British Mandate power and also against any Arabs that opposed the founding of a Jewish national state with weapons in their hands. The protection of the settlements was taken over by the Haganah, which itself refrained from any acts of terror. And what were the British colonial rulers doing at the time? They were "catching" the members of the armed self-defense organizations "in the act," confiscating, wherever possible, all weapons, throwing the fighters into prison. The country was like a witches' cauldron.

In the meantime, detention camps in Germany were being filled with Jews liberated from the concentration camps in Eastern Europe and Germany. But Great Britain turned down the suggestion of the American President Truman that Palestine take in 100,000 Jews. The situation was heating up, inside and out. And we can only cite, in deep mourning for the constantly-repeated reluctance of the world to bring Jews back to life, what Arthur D. Morse observed in his book "While 6 Million Died – A Chronicle of American Apathy": Great Britain and the U.S.A. could have helped in the flight of Jews from Europe, but they intentionally avoided doing so until almost the end of the war!

Finally, in the spring of 1947, the government in London decided to relinquish its Mandate. It brought the problem of Palestine, which it could not cope with, before the United Nations. A special commission composed of statesmen and jurists from eleven member nations of the United Nations recommended the partition of Palestine into one Jewish state and one Arab state, which would be part of an economic union, with Jerusalem under international control. On November 29th, 1947, the General Assembly of the United Nations approved this recommendation with more than the required two-thirds majority. Both the United States and the Soviet Union supported the resolution.

The decision was accepted by the Jewish Agency, but was rejected by the Arab governments and the Palestinian leaders. The six months before the end of the British Mandate were marked by acts of violence by the Arabs on the Jewish community. The Arabs attempted to disrupt communication between the Jewish cities and villages and, above all, to isolate and conquer Jerusalem. Before the invasion of the country by the Arab armies in April of 1948, however, they did not succeed in occupying a single Jewish town or city, although the British authorities were helping the Arabs by handing over military positions and equipment. British officers commanded the Trans-Jordan Arab Legion.

On May 14th, 1948 (5th of Iyar, 5708), the new Jewish State could finally be proclaimed. A democracy had been created, one which, in the time to come, was to prove a bastion of the free West. The language of the Constitution, its contents and its instructions for the political future are proof that modern Israel was born a democracy. The decision pronounced on that day, to found a Jewish State, was reached not only in full agreement of the United Nations, but also, a fact which is often neglected, through a democratically-elected leadership of the Zionist organization, which represented Jews all over the world, as well as through an elected parliament (Asefat ha'Nivharim), the organization that represented Jews in Palestine. Both bodies had long years of experience in democratic self-government at their disposal, with their political parties, which represented the will of the people. Before the end of the British Mandate, it was possible to organize a national assembly and a national governing body which could set up the groundwork for the government to come.

The Declaration of Independence of the State of Israel of the 14th of May reads, in part.

"It is the natural right of the Jewish people, as of all other peoples, to command its fate under its own sovereignty."
"The State of Israel stands

open to Jewish immigration
and to the gathering of
Jews living in exile. It will
dedicate itself to opening
the land to the good of all
its inhabitants."

"It will rest upon the principles
of freedom, justice, and
peace, in the spirit of the
prophets."

"It will guarantee to its
citizens social and political
equality, without distinctions
based on religion, race,
or sex. It will assure freedom
of conscience as well as
freedom of speech and
culture. It will take the holy
sites under its protection
and will remain true to the
principles of the Charter of
the United Nations.

"We reach out our hand to all our neighboring countries and their peoples for peace and neighborly coexistence."

In 1950, this Charter was supplemented by the Return Law, which conforms to the principle allowing every Jew, upon entering the country, to become a citizen of Israel.

Although with this declaration, from the first days of the Jewish State on, the hands of peace had been stretched out toward its neighbors, never during its new existence has it known true peace. Not a single day has gone by on which Arab acts of terrorism were not carried out. Not a single day has been free from the danger of becoming victim to violent Arab plots.

In the 24 hours after the proclamation, the people that were from that moment on Israelis saw the last British troops pull out, taking all their bag and baggage with them, board ship, and leave Palestine. No one shed a tear. The joy was great; the fate of the country was in the hands of those remaining behind, who were full of hope for the future. A dream had become a reality.

On the very day the nation was founded, well-equipped and trained armies from Egypt, Trans-Jordan, Iraq, Lebanon, and Saudi Arabia invaded the area that from that hour on had come to be called Israel. The Arab attack succeeded in capturing land, because the small country had not been made the land of the Jews for strategic reasons. Its borders, with the exception of the Mediterranean coast, ran along contrary to strategic conditions, dictated by the trend decided at the round table, separating, insofar as possible, Arab and Jewish settlements. At one point, there were less than 10 miles between Trans-Jordan and the coast. Israel became the land of minimal distances; mountains and plains, cities and towns, verdant fields and uncultivated deserts lay only a few miles from one another.

Characteristic of the prevailing attitude in the Arab states from the first day on – which still remains unchanged – is that on the very day Ben-Gurion proclaimed the founding of the State, the General Secretary of the Arab League, Azzam Pasha, loudly announced, after the attack, "This is going to be a war of extermination and a powerful massacre which people will speak of as they do of the massacres of the Mongolians and the crusaders."

Although the Egyptian army at first succeeded in reaching a point 20 miles south of Tel Aviv, Arab troops laid siege to Jerusalem, the Iraqis had already pushed through toward the coast to a distance of less than 10 miles from the Mediterranean, which precipitated the danger that Israel would be cut in half, and the Syrian enemy was moving in a westward direction in Upper Galilee, the scantily-armed, numerically much weaker Israeli military groups succeeded in fighting off the invading armies. In this War for Independence, which could only be ended by the signing of a cease-fire treaty with Egypt, Jordan, Lebanon, and Syria, 6000 Israelis were killed. The sacrifice was tremendous. But the hostility the Israelis

were exposed to did not
end. The Arab politicians
have never hidden their
intention of destroying the
Jewish State, although
certainly more than once
they must have seen cause
to recognize that it is not
up to them alone to realize
this goal. They practice
propaganda, with which
they systematically rouse
naked hate among the
population of their nations
and abroad, where their
influence is constantly
increasing, and try to deface
the true picture of Israel,
the picture of unwavering
hope in the peaceful con-
struction of their country.
This policy reached a climax
in 1956. The Arabs attacked
Israel again. This gave

way to the Sinai War, which lasted from October 29th until November 5th, 1956.

Egyptian President Nasser could not resign himself to the defeat. On May 25th, 1965, together with the Iraqi president, among others, he published a declaration with a tone of irreconcilable enmity: "The Arab national goal is the extermination of Israel." Tension in the Middle East escalated, so that Israel was forced to take preventive measures. The situation itself was overripe. In the Six Day War (June 5–11, 1967), after hoping for three weeks for international intervention, Israel destroyed the Arab troops deployed on her borders, which threatened her very existence. Despite their defeat, Israel's Arab neighboring countries could not accept the situation. One act of terror after another followed. The method of their constant escalation was called: massacre!

It came in 1973. On the highest Jewish holiday, called the Day of Atonement, on October 6th, 1973, as a peaceful holiday spirit lay over the whole land of Israel, Egypt and Syria attacked Israel's national borders simultaneously. The attack came unexpectedly and at a moment when Israel was not at all in a state of full vigilance and readiness, let alone mobilization.

Just the same, the rapidly-called-up army succeeded in bringing the enemy armies' drive to a halt in a matter of a few days and even to establish a bridgehead on the other side of the Suez Canal and to make large advances in the Golan Heights.

In this war, the Arab states had brought a weapon into action that they had not used before, the weapon "oil." This product, of vital importance to the western nations, was used as a method of strangulation. Oil-exporting Arab states put into effect a progressive reduction in total production, and a total embargo on deliveries to the United States and the Netherlands, on the pretext that they were pro-Israeli. Western Europe seemed to be thrown to the mercy of the oil sheiks and was not able to present a unified front.

On October 22nd, 1973, the United Nations Security Council formally adopted a resolution (No. 338), after the war on the Middle East fronts had turned to Israel's favor and after the American Secretary of State had been hurriedly invited to Moscow. The United Nations resolution recommended the cessation of hostilities and the enforcement of the resolution of November 22nd, 1967. The fighting continued for another 36 hours, followed, after an oft-broken cease-fire, by the signing of a Six-Point Agreement between Israel and Egypt, and later by a troop disengagement agreement also between Israel and Syria. Between the fronts patrolled a hastily-put-together United Nations force. A Middle East peace conference assembled on December 21st in Geneva. Steering the Israeli ship of state through all these complications in international as well as domestic policy proved to be extremely complicated, all the more so because Israeli public opinion is split into so many parties.

The focal point of democratic

life in Israel has, of course, become the Knesset, the Parliament. Its members mould the parliamentary life of the country, which two political groups would especially like to get into their hands: on one side the hawks, who are relentlessly opposed to concessions to the enemy, especially in regard to the areas won in the Six Day War, and the doves, who are ready to compromise, in order, above all, to reach a peace with the Arab neighbors.

The Israeli population, which in 1972 amounted to about 3,200,500, has many faces. Figures give a glimpse: 27.1% come from Europe and America; 25.7% from Asia

and Africa; the rest are
mainly Sabras, with a small
percentage coming from
other countries, which, in
the course of time, has
changed the picture on
Israeli streets. A visible
Orientalizing has developed,
which continues to increase.
Not only is the problem
of integrating immigrants from
the various countries
growing, but the immigration
of Soviet Jews has recently
brought up complicated
questions, to an extent
because these immigrants
frequently are not able
to compose a true picture for
themselves of life in Israel.
In their homeland, the Soviet
Union, no such information
is available, so that they
develop an idealistically-

tinged image. Then come the facts – that they do not understand Hebrew, one of the national languages – the other is Arabic – and that they have the impractical wish – which one can fully understand in view of their situation – not to be separated from their Soviet fellow-believers, the people with whom they shared their existence in the threatening struggle to immigrate to Israel and with whom they have lived. In addition, many of them have professions which are not in demand in Israel or which are already overcrowded. So they are, of necessity, subject to re-schooling, in order to be able to become integrated into Israeli life. The country, clearly geared to immigration, should, however, be able to master these difficulties.

There is hardly a problem in Israel – and it is unfortunately not exactly lacking in problems – that has proved so difficult to solve as the integration of the Arabs in Israel. In the Declaration of Independence, they are designated as "members of the Arab people." They are recognized as a separate national group, whose members, however, have the right to the same citizenship and representation in national institutions. No attempt will ever be made to assimilate the Arabs, to dispute their nationality, or to prevent them from developing their own culture, language, or religion. Since 1967, numerous Jewish-Arab groups have been formed for the promotion of social contact between Jews and Arabs. They have played a great part toward the reduction of the myths and clichés built up during the many years of conflict.

Then came the 13th of November, 1974, the day on which Yasir Arafat, leader of the terroristic, murder- and manslaughter-propagating, so-called Palestine Liberation Organization (PLO), stood before the United Nations and, to applause such as has never before been heard in the General Assembly, was permitted to proclaim his misanthropic doctrine. Since that day, November 13th, 1974, the United Nations bears the disgraceful stigma of being a tool of barbarism.

The conflict situation between the Arabs' sense of belonging to the country in which they live and their feeling of belonging to the Arab people had become explosive. Fear of later reprisals on the part of the Palestinians had reached a climax; they did not want – justified or not – to fall under suspicion and be considered collaborators of Israel. A false pride was stirred up, urging them to belong to the power group, now not called Israel, but the "Palestine Liberation Organization".

Perhaps it will eventually be the Arab woman who will come closer to European-thinking Israel and will thereby lead the way to change. But it still holds true that her word has no weight, or at least not much, in a family in which the husband and father is the total dictator. In status, in fact, the mother comes after the husband, even after the sons and daughters.

The personal status of the Arab woman in Israel has changed considerably in the course of less than 30 years, a generation. Bigamy is forbidden by law, although

the Moslem religious laws
permit it. Israeli law also
forbids child marriages; the
minimum age for marriage
of women is 17. The woman's
consent to the marriage
is required by law, and an
adult woman is not required
to obtain permission to
marry from her guardian.
A significant change, in
regard to the legal status of
the woman, was the estab-
lishment of the law forbidding
divorce without the woman's
consent. The path from
feudalism to the pluralistic
society is open!

Women's legal status has
also changed for the better.
The first clause of the 1951
law on equality for women
stipulates: "The same laws

are to be applied in the same way to men and women in all legal matters, and those laws which discriminate against women may not be administered." The equality of women naturally also grants political and civil rights to the Arab woman. This has come to be a reality in Israeli life: every Arab woman over 18 years of age has, like her Jewish Israeli counterpart, the right to vote. It has been proven that Arab women do use their right to vote and participate, in increasing numbers, in public, social, and political activities. Several Arab villages have women's councils and clubs, which organize lectures and study days and are also politically active. So the emancipation of the Arab woman has already made a certain amount of progress.

The attitude of another minority, the Druses, is quite different. They have become a part of life in the State of Israel. Their identification with the country was clearly demonstrated by their faithful service in the security troops. Many Druse soldiers and officers lost their lives in the fight for the survival of Israel. Military service is obligatory for them. However, parallel with their integration, they have been able, through special courts of law and through their special way of life, to retain their religious identity and common traits.

Arabs and Druses, as well as members of other minorities, are permitted to serve in on the police force. Of the 12,850 men and women that compose it, according to the statistics of 1972, 1200 are Arabs and Druses.

A duty of the Israeli police apparatus that is unknown in other countries is the guarding of cease-fire lines against terrorist infiltration from neighboring countries. Some of the women enlisted for military service are assigned to police duty in Jerusalem, Tel Aviv, and Haifa. The picture of Israeli female traffic-control police-women is already an every-day matter.

The protection of the State requires a maximum-trained defense system with modern equipment constantly ready for action. The military force emerged from the Haganah and other volunteer underground movements which were formed during the Mandate era, as well as the veterans of the Jewish Brigade and other military units that battled on the side of the Allies in the Second World War.

The population and economic potential of Israel opposes the maintenance of a profes-sional army. The constant danger of possible acts of aggression, however, necessitated the search for a solution – which was found, although it is somewhat unusual. A standing army, intentionally called defense army, was formed, consisting of a relatively small nucleus of professional officers, non-commissioned officers, and soldiers. In addition, there is a contingent of soldiers who are drafted in fulfillment of their military duty according to the draft law. But the main body of this army consists of reservists. The law allows for the enlistment of men up to 55 years of age and of women without children up to 34 in the reserve. On this basis, men are called up for reserve duty 30 days per year. Married and pregnant women, as well as mothers, are, however, exempt from military service. Women may also be released on the basis of religious conviction by consent of a combined civilian-military committee.

It is due to the willingness of Israeli youth to risk their own lives, if necessary, to protect their country, the lives of their families, and the existence of the entire population that, out of a small standing army, a mighty civilian army can be instantaneously formed. This may not only be due to a deep and highly developed sense of patriotism, but also to the fact that the relationship between officers and soldiers is different from that which is usual in other armies. Formal rank is less important than ability, personality, and leadership.

Leadership is, moreover, expressed through personal example, rather than by the power to give orders.

An organization which is often criticized abroad, and that because of ignorance of the needs that arise in Israel, is the Nachal (No'ar Chaluzi Lohem), the fighting pioneer youth. This is a specially-formed corps, formed for security reasons especially in border areas, which combines military training with pioneer work and agri-cultural training. This group is engaged during the construction of new settle-ments along the border or, if settlements are to be founded in areas that are too dangerous for civilians, they found the settlements themselves. When the Nachal group, composed of men and women, has completed its work and the settlement no longer needs help, their job is done. Then the Nachal pioneer becomes a civilian like any other.

For boys and girls from 14 to 18 years old, there is a youth corps, Gadna (Gedudei No'ar), which is under the combined jurisdiction of the Ministries of Defense and Education. These young people receive training in pioneering, and special sections are able to obtain training for the air force and navy. This pre-military youth organization, active during and after school, is for the most part involved with nature, although the members are subject to military training in various branches of service.

The Chen (Cheil Naschim), a military assistance organization for women, supports the defense army in many respects. Women generally fulfill un-armed duties, ranging from radio to hospital work to teaching, the idea being to reduce the workload on the men in the army.

Here the question obviously arises of whether the various minorities are drafted or allow themselves to be drafted for the national defense. Members of minorities can, under certain circumstances, enlist as volunteers; that is, only when they themselves wish to. For example, as already mentioned, many Druses have reached officer rank. Bedouins and members of the Christian-Arabic community can also enlist as volunteers; they then serve in a special unit for Druses and Christian Arabs. This unit has served well in many border maneuvers. Terrorism on the part of Palestinians after the Yom Kippur War also made it necessary for so-called militias, composed mainly of older men, to be formed in many border cities, towns, and settlements.

Olivier Todd, Chief Editor of

the 'Nouvel Observateur,'
commented as follows on
the Israeli army after the Yom
Kippur War:

"The 'Arab World' boasts
with militarism, the childhood
disease of nationalism and
underdevelopment. Israel,
isolated and security-
conscious as she is, possesses
a civilian army equal to the
revolutionary Jacobin dream.
The Israeli defense army is
politically conscious, not
to say saturated with political
commissaries. In fact, this
is probably the only military
organization in the world
that can truly claim the so –
often misused attribute of
'popular.' Legends have
arisen, the Israeli defense
fighters often portrayed as

blind centurions. But when the whole story of this fourth war has been written – a war fought to protect the Jewish State – it will become clear that the Jewish soldier is very familiar with fear...

"True, the Israeli defense army has its share of coarse sergeants and pigheaded colonels. But for the most part the brotherly atmosphere that prevails here is, in comparison to the social inflexibility of the Arab armies, very much to their favor. Everywhere in the world, the Left has difficulties in defining its attitude toward the military. The Israeli defense force is undoubtedly a particularly confusing phenomenon.

The extreme Left, wishing to press the Palestinian question and help the Israeli Left, should, before anything else, ask itself a question: Is it not true that partisan hostility against Israel, with all its civil and military aspects, is caused by a subconscious anti-Semitism, masked as anti-Zionism? This is a question that particularly Leftists that are Jewish should ask themselves. Masochism is often a major part of a hard political line."

This draws our attention at the same time to a political phenomenon which exists in Israel, just as in the rest of the world. And why not? Among the young, there are always groups prone to extremes, which, for a time – consciously or unconsciously – follow a path which would destroy their very existence.

From the beginning on, a problem, indeed a particularly Israeli problem, has been the integration of immigrants. Israel has become a melting pot of some 70 nations. To the army has fallen the special mission, not only of building military units, but also of bringing about social unity. Under no circumstances were or are the differences in intellectual, cultural, or economic levels to act divisively.

Integration of the immigrants into Israeli life? From 1948 to the present, Israel's population has grown to nearly five times its original size, as shown by the following figure from 1972: 3,200,500 inhabitants. That means 1,400,000 immigrants in 24 years!

The two basic needs of the immigrant on arrival are: shelter and work. During the first three years, in which immigration doubled the population, the country, which had surmounted a hard War of Independence, was still in its baby shoes, and its economy was in poor shape. Most of the immigrants were housed in tent-camps, the "Ma'abarot" – provisional living areas with primitive shelters. Conditions were difficult,

employment often scarcely to be obtained, and many immigrants were forced to live on welfare or to earn their living by working at public welfare activities. Today the newcomers are brought directly to new apartments or classification centers, where they learn Hebrew. Most of them do find work.

Education is one of the most important responsibilities, one Israel could never ignore, not only for the newcomers, but also for those (Sabras) born in Israel. That the importance of education is recognized by the State is substantiated by the fact that expenditures for education occupy the third largest place in the national budget, following those for defense and housing.

Elementary and secondary education are free of charge and fall under the general Compulsory Education Act. Educational reform has raised the compulsory school age to 16. The largest educational problem is that of closing the gap between children with European-American backgrounds and children from Asian-African countries. Between 1956-57 and 1969-70, the number of children from Asiatic and African homes attending secondary schools rose 35%.

Higher education is rooted in the fact that Israel is a

small country and relatively poor in natural resources. To make up for this insufficiency, great stress is placed on the development of human abilities and the training of highly qualified scholars, skilled laborers, scientists, and engineers. It has been reported that at the time the country was founded it possessed two universities, in which a total of 1788 students were enrolled. Today there are seven such institutions, with more than 45,000 students, among them many foreigners. Some 75% of their budget is financed by the government and the Jewish Agency, while the remaining 25% comes from private sources, mainly contributions from abroad and tuition.

The tourist visiting Israel, the land of miracles come true, never gets over his astonishment and admiration. And not only because he can see with his own eyes how, out of the wasteland, wooded land and fertile fields have grown, villages become towns and these become cities, where life pulsates just as it does in the North, East, West, or South of the earth. Where once traders, caravans, and camels loaded with goods, had to trudge their weary way, today a broad, modern transportation system winds through the land.

Decades ago, as the first oak trees flourished in a kibbutz near the road leading from Haifa to Nazareth, a young girl said to Henrietta Szold, mother of the Children's and Youth Aliyah, whose mission was to rescue children from burning Europe and bring them to Palestine, that the trees in her native German homeland were more beautiful, the foliage more lusciously green, the leaves more characteristically jagged. And how did Henrietta Szold answer? She said, "Not more beautiful, just – different!" The traveler in Israel learns the deep meaning of this assertion. Things are not always necessarily more beautiful, just – well, just different. The Israelis, the Sabra and the new arrival, are equally proud of their country, because of its uniqueness, its – being different.

Can't he experience pride, for example, in the fact that the number of books published in his country – per capita – takes second place in the world? The people who gave the Bible to the civilized world have become the people of readers. To meet an Israeli who does not have a book collection is a rarity. Two thousand libraries with approximately 13 million books speak eloquently for the reading habits of these education-hungry people. Among them has arisen a new generation of writers who primarily write in Hebrew. In their works, they treat the substance of present-day Israel, as well as current world problems. All of Israeli literature felt honored at the awarding of the Nobel Prize for Literature 1966 to the Hebrew poet Agnon. (He shared the prize, as is well known, with the German-born Jewish poetess Nelly Sachs, singer of sorrows and reconciliation.)

Art is written with a capital letter, because in artistic spheres Israel reveals noteworthy and many-sided activity.
The Jewish State has many artists who have made a name for themselves – as is shown by the extraordinarily

high number of authorities
in the area of theater, music,
and painting, as well as
other arts, at all times and
all over the world, particularly
in Central Europe.

Theater enjoys particular
popularity in Israel. The
season lasts eleven months,
and sometimes there are
even performances during
the vacation month, August –
the dream of all theater
directors abroad. Actor and
theater director Joseph Milo,
born in Prague, once re-
ported that in a single
season three and a half
million tickets had been sold
– not given away!

The vitality of theater life in
Israel is exceeded still by

that of the musicians. In 1936, the world-famous violinist Bronislaw Huberman founded the Israel Philharmonic Orchestra and convinced Maestro Arturo Toscanini to direct. To date this remains the most significant musical ensemble in Israel. With 32,000 subscribers, it holds, per capita, a world record. It does not, however, stand alone in Israel's musical life. A series of orchestras, the Israel National Opera, the Chamber Music Ensemble, which has also played guest appearances abroad with great success, hardly play second fiddle to them. Good choruses exist in all cities, some of which have, like the dance groups, won great acclaim abroad. Musical life is enriched by the numerous works by Israeli composers, and folk songs and dances are very popular. Some popular singers have also attained high rank in the musical world.

Highly talented artists are to be found among the Israeli painters. The mode of painting is not as closely related to the Paris School as it is to the Eastern European, just as in the theater the influence of Stanislavski, Tairoff, or Reinhardt can be observed. Abstract painting serves as an unexpected analogy to the Old Testament tradition which, at least in the synagogue, forbids the image of man in art.

A country, says one expert, in which routine and speculation are worth so little, doesn't exactly make things easy in the arts. And it is not only the political situation that takes so much of one's vital energy; this is a special style of life, which requires almost all of one's strength.

Over 20 feature-length films are made yearly. Their number is climbing, as is the number of shorts and television films. 260 motion picture theaters with some 180,000 seats show the amount of interest in this area of the arts.

Radio and the press play a significant role. The style and nature of good European journalism has been retained here. Infringements on freedom of the press do, however, occur. Censorship can be invoked; the politically precarious situation seems to be more important than a free journalistic news service and commentary. The board of censors consists of three members: one representative of the army, one representative of the newspaper publishers, and one representative of the public – the composition of the group shows its aims. Decisions can only be reached by a majority!

Sports? Naturally they exist, too, in the land of the Maccabees. King Soccer also reigns in the Holy Land, though only as an amateur sport. But just the same, at the Olympics – what a bitter after-taste that word has taken on since the murder of eleven members of the Israeli delegation at the games in Munich – the Israelis dared to compete with the professionals. In 1970, the amateurs of the soccer midgets qualified for the world championship in Mexico. The results: a 0-0 score wrung from Italy, 1-1 from Sweden. – Other popular sports in which Israelis are particularly active are swimming, track and field, tennis, rowing, sailing, basketball, handball, and volleyball, as well as fencing, gymnastics, weightlifting, and wrestling. Variety is also valued and encouraged in this area. The Maccabean Games are held every four years, the first series having been held in 1932 in Tel Aviv. They bring together Jewish athletes for an Olympics-like competition.

"Tradition, Tradition" is the name of the song from the musical "Fiddler on the Roof." Wherever you go in Israel, you run into this Tradition. And this does not only apply to religion. There is also an ancient agricultural tradition.

Historically, the Jews emerged as a nomadic people which, like the Bedouins, was chiefly engaged in sheep and goat breeding. The Bible describes the Jews as

a folk of farmers and fisher-
men. Today, in Israel, it has
come to be recognized that
agriculture is not only the
most important basis, but
also a difficult task for a
people that has lived primarily in cities for so many
centuries. The conception of
the money-making branches
of the economy yielded to
the demands of agriculture,
in which the farmers could
themselves produce the food
they needed for their own
sustenance: grain, vegetables,
dairy products. So emerged
the plan to construct the
social structure of the village
around self-sufficient labor
and to divide the land so
that no one would need to
work as a paid laborer,
but that, with the help of

women and children, they could do everything themselves. This led to the development of the cooperative and collective idea, which was put into practice in the form of moshavot and kibbutzim.

The kibbutz in Israel presents a unique social form, on the basis of its social structure and its way of life. Its most striking characteristic is based upon the willingness of its members to join in a society which is never limited to a chosen circle of people and which is constantly growing. Since the modest beginnings in 1909 with eight members, the kibbutz movement has grown to 80,000. The settlers of the moshavot and the kibbutzim exercise a great deal of leadership in all areas, particularly in the political, cultural, and military.

"Is the member of the kibbutz only a number, one of many? Doesn't he have to relinquish his own personality for the good of the community? Doesn't communal life automatically place large restraints on personal development?" These and similar questions have been asked abroad for decades; they have not yet died out. No one lives in a vacuum. Every society, no matter what form it takes, must place certain limitations on its members. Through this means, the kibbutz also exercises its protective measures in the area of

economic and social equalizing, just as a democracy only considers limitations justified if they are necessary to protect the citizen against threats from within or without. In Israel, one can convince oneself: the kibbutz grants its members the complete and unlimited democratic right of co-determination in all decisions of a community nature.
Of course the following also holds true for the social framework of the kibbutz: Every society consists of living people, and every person has his faults.

Many guests from all over the world visit and work on the kibbutzim, which from the very beginning have had a magnetic power of attraction for outsiders. Recently young people from the Federal Republic of Germany have also been admitted, against which many kibbutzim had fought for a long time.

Recent times have shown a swing from the agricultural collectives to industry, to urban economic life, although the business situation, which had taken a large upswing in more than two decades, has become more and more difficult, no differently than it has in the western nations. A few figures reflect the rapid economic growth: Between 1952 and 1970, the gross national product was multi-

plied by nearly six. In 1972,
it amounted to 2200 dollars
per capita, almost three
times as much as in 1950
(859 dollars). To compare:
In 1952, Israel's gross
national product amounted
to half that of Egypt; in 1972,
the G.N.P. was the same
in both countries!

Immigration resulted in a
boom in the building industry,
which occupies a central
role in the Israeli economy.
Of significance for the
country was the fact that it
was able to succeed in
quickly raising the necessary
capital abroad. Between
1948 and 1970, transfers of
capital reached a total
of 12,000 million dollars.
This came primarily from

three sources: contributions
and investments by Jews
abroad, reparation payments
from West Germany, and
loans from foreign governments.

Many branches of industry
literally grew out of the
earth. The political situation
made it necessary to also
build up a defense-linked
industry, particularly for the
manufacturing of parts for
complex weapons.

But a particular problem has
been growing in the
economy. Israel has consist-
ently been forced to import
more than it can export.
There has therefore been a
consistent trade deficit, which
has had to be covered by

the importation of capital. The State has indeed made considerable progress in increasing its exports, as is proven by the following figures: 1950 – 35 million dollars; 1971 – 957 million dollars. In the same period of time, however, imports also grew considerably and, in 1970, reached a height of 1808 million dollars, of which a large share fell to defense requirements. In 1971, the trade deficit reached 851 million dollars; the trend is rising.

Israel's national budget cannot be met solely by the high taxes that have to be imposed on its citizens; it also depends on the generosity of Jews abroad. The American Jews, who have been constantly on the spot to offer help since the time of the Russian pogroms, as well as the heterogenously-composed Jewish community in West Germany, lead in the financial sacrifices offered by the Jews of the world for the Jewish State. The Jews of the world are clearly aware of Israel's importance for their own existence and demonstrate this.

The founding of Israel was a bit of epic poetry and an act of political imagination, but it was not a well-thought-out act in view of the world as it actually is. The foundation and construction of the Jewish State have proven what powers and abilities lay within the Jews and then became reality. But reality, as opposed to fantasy, has limitations, although it is just this fantasy which is necessary to achieve the reality. This makes all the difference. The rise of the State of Israel has shown this.

On May 11th, 1949, as Israel was accepted into the United Nations, it looked as though that country had finally taken its place among the peoples of the earth and was recognized as equal and incontestable. Since then, the situation has changed radically, especially after the Yom Kippur War and even though Israel resisted making a preventive attack on the troops which had gathered at its borders.

Balaam's statement has become the naked reality: "Look, a people, one that lives separated from other peoples, but is not counted among the peoples." Israel is isolated. Today, right now, in the General Assembly of the United Nations.

With anxious hearts, Israelis and their few friends in the outside world ask the question: How will the future of this nation be shaped, a land which in its develop-ment strives more strongly than ever to attain peace, a peace it must reach within just, secured borders, if it is to emerge from the dilemma that hostile neighbors and the rest of the callous world have imposed on it since the day it was founded. Will America, one day when its foreign and domestic political situations require it, break its promise to maintain the military balance in the Middle East via shipments of armaments to the threatened State?

Finally, some significant statements by prominent Israelis:

The former Minister of Information, Aharon Yariv, said in an interview: "The subjective feeling of power is more important than the objective development. From this standpoint,

it is certain that the Arabs
scored a victory (in the
Yom Kippur War). As far as
our feelings and outlook are
concerned, we emerged
weaker. Sadat was recently
asked: 'Did you win the
war?' He answered: 'Look at
what is happening in Israel!'
I am sorry to say that a
large gap exists between
our image in our own eyes
and our actual strength.
In the fifties, there was a gap
between our strength and
our self-image. At that time
we had more confidence in
our strength, and our image
was much greater than our
actual strength. Unfortunately
the opposite is true in 1974."

This is a clear criticism,
particularly to the hawks.

It should not die away unheeded.

President Yitzhak Rabin was asked by Dov Goldstein of "Ma'ariv" in an interview at the end of 1974: "Can you tell us what you would do if you were to be plunged into another war under the circumstances of the Yom Kippur War?"

The President answered in part: "I would like to be frank: The fact that their armies consist of regular troops and that it is not necessary to mobilize reservists gives the Arabs a certain advantage and the ability to surprise us. Above all, we must return to the Ben-Gurion doctrine: 'Never underestimate the enemy.' On the other hand, we should remember that, despite the initial situation in the Yom Kippur War, the Israeli army was able to turn the tide in its favor within a few days. In the memory of the Arabs, as in ours, the image of the first three days is firmly anchored, whereas the way the war ended is completely ignored. Perhaps the Arabs are right. It is in their interest to remember the first three days. We should not forget them; however, there is no reason that we should not also remember the end of the war, today, as we are armed against danger and know that Israel's army commands strong combat forces, able to defend us against the aggressor. Our enemies should know this, too."

This is clear language, which should be understood everywhere, although it must be emphasized again that the opinion of the Israelis on the question of the return of the territory occupied since the Six Day War has fundamentally changed. The doves have — or so it seems, at least — achieved a majority over the hawks. They are for peace with compromise, whereas the others are still prepared to fight to the bitter end, no matter how it might turn out for Israel, because they have absolute confidence in the might of the defense army and in the

ability of the Israelis in open battle.

In an interview at about the same time, the Minister of Defense, Simon Peres, said, after having commented that the State of Israel had a deficit of 5 million dollars and the Arabs, in contrast, a surplus of 4.5 million dollars:
"We collect large contributions from our brothers all over the world — and then King Faisal comes to Cairo, hears one single speech — and draws a checkbook out and throws in 100 million dollars."

And on the subject of the oil crisis, which forced many western nations to kowtow to the oil sheiks, the Minister said:

"If it should come to another oil crisis, it would be desirable if its victims were to be better prepared and less tolerant than during the preceding crisis. I believe that the oil affair not only is an external problem, but also points up internal problems. Many thousands of Arab students have asked themselves whether the entire oil profit is really intended for Cadillacs and princely palaces or whether it isn't also meant to fill other functions in Arab history and in the economy of the Arab world."

The great question mark remains. There may be many answers, with subjective, individual characters. The politicians, and not only Israelis, but also Arab politicians and those of the Great Powers, naturally consider the national interests of their countries first; but one or another of them just might also have a conception of the whole. Today, tomorrow, the day after tomorrow, even many years from now, the prophets may still be interpreting and arguing over the way to a solution of the problems in the Middle East. All Israelis and their friends will come to the conviction that the experience of thousands of years has proven: The people of Israel will live on.

As varied as their customs and lands of origin are, something dreamlike-Chassidic clings to all Israelis, even though they also know how to grab hold and fight whenever it is necessary. They believe in miracles, in fairy tales, and, with the work of their own hands and much spiritual and material sacrifice, with tenacity of purpose, they have realized Theodor Herzl's call to action: If you want it, it is no fairy tale!

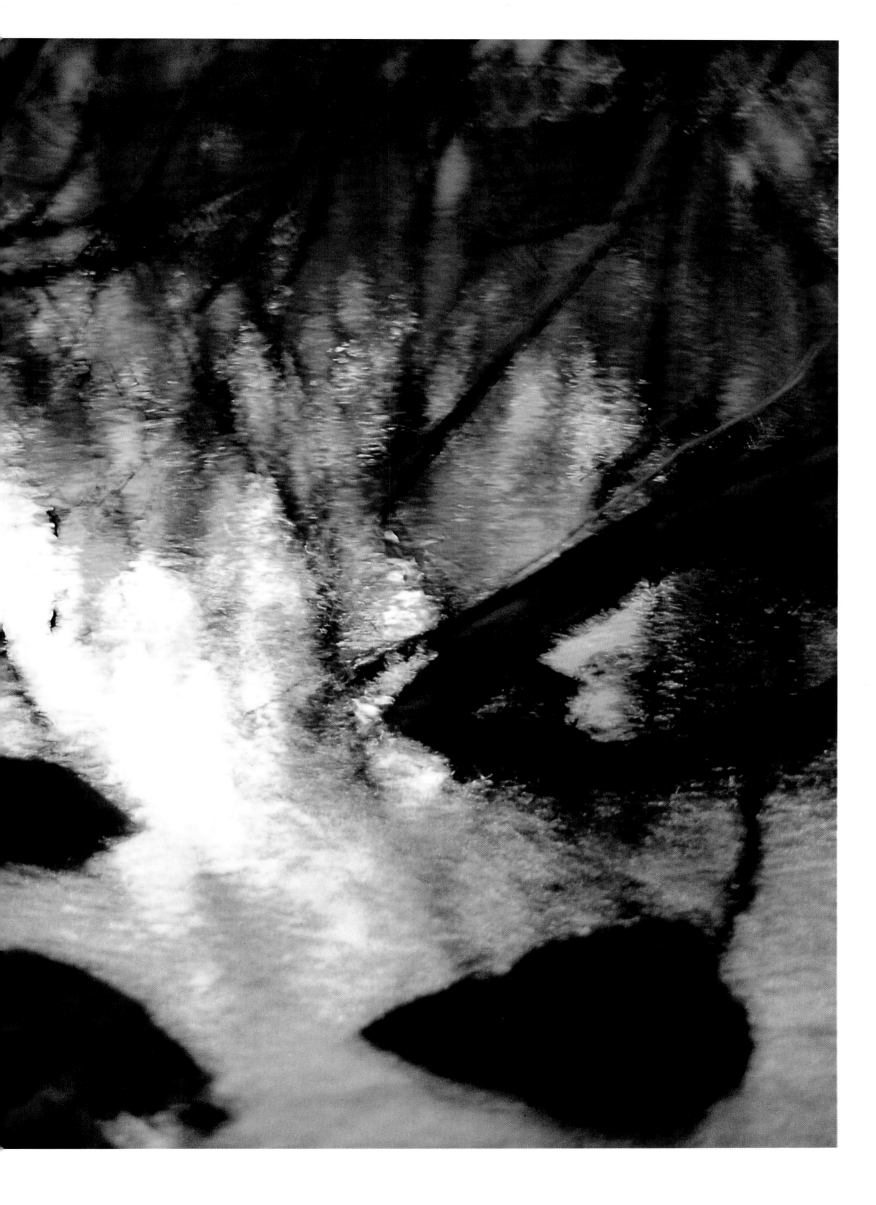

85
86-87 In April of 1973, I made my first trip to Israel. For many years, I had wanted to learn to know this land, but books about Japan and Mexico stood in the way of this project. The timing of my trip was carefully planned: During my visit Israel celebrated the 25th anniversary of its founding. Joy and reflection balanced one another. Driving from Tel Aviv to Jerusalem, I saw, at the foot of a steep slope, the gutted, since rusted remains of military vehicles, witnesses of the struggle for this city. With national flags and flowers, the citizens had made war memorials out of these rusted objects.

88-89 High above Jerusalem lies the cemetery of fallen Israeli soldiers. On May 7th, 1973, Golda Meir talks about Israel's struggle for freedom and about the many young Israelis who paid for this freedom with their lives. Yet her words cannot comfort these mothers.

90-91 Golda Meir remembers the dead. The many dead. On the 25th anniversary of the founding of the State of Israel.

92-93 On the Golan Heights, I photographed this impro-vised memorial, constructed out of steel helmets, machine gun belts, stones, cutlery, and shoes.

94-95 In front of the Knesset, the Israeli parliament building in

Jerusalem, stands a huge seven-armed candelabrum, decorated with scenes from the history of the suffering of the Jewish people. A gift from the English government.

96-97
98-99
100-101
The Israel Museum in Jerusalem is a symbol of the will to live of the Jewish people: besieged, burdened with incredibly high expenditures for defense, this people managed to create for itself a place of cultural statement of incomparable diversity. On the occasion of its opening, the Museum received presents from all spheres of the arts. But the main emphasis of the Israel Museum is its collection of archeology and Jewish ceremonial art. Here, in close proximity, one can compare ceremonial objects of the same type, stemming from the most diverse countries where Jews have taken root in the past centures. The photos show Torah-cases, marriage contracts, a menorah from the 18th century, a detail of the robes of Jewish women from Bukhara, as well as other examples from the archeological and folklore sections.

102-103
In May of 1973, I roamed through the verdant land, experienced Israel's checkered landscape: wonderful sand beaches, fruitful vineyards and plantations, desert areas, and steep mountains.

104-105
The Jordan – its source.

106-107　With the greatest speed, the spring waters of the Jordan swell to form a river, agilely rushing along. Its waters hurry along for some 170 miles, finally to empty into the Dead Sea.

108-109　Approximately 300,000 spectators pack the streets of Jerusalem for the parade celebrating the 25th anniversary of the founding of the nation. A formation of Fouga-Magister planes, leaving blue-white trails of smoke behind them, opens the fly-past of the air force. Helicopters follow, then twenty-five Fouga-Magisters in a formation forming the letters Kaf-Heh, which means 25 in Hebrew. After that come bombers of American origin, two groups of French Super-Mistères, as well as the super-fast Phantom planes. The wild humming has hardly died down when the motorized units appear: Centurion tanks, then a unit of Pattons M48/A3. After that comes a second group of battle tanks, equipped with the most modern equipment, for example, with infra-red telescopic sights. The tank column is followed by the artillery. Here the Howitzer L 33/155 tank is the great attraction. These guns have been manufactured in Israel and are being shown for the very first time. Then comes the air force convoy. Here the group of 40-caliber Bofors anti-aircraft guns and a group of

American-made Hawk rockets stands out. At the end are marching troops of parachute jumpers, soldiers from all branches of service, soldiers from the minority groups – Druses and Circassians – as well as the military police. At 11:30, after 1½ hours, the greatest military parade Israel has ever staged has come to an end, without incident.

110-111 Packed closely together, the flag-bearers march past the commanding general in charge, Prime Minister Golda Meir, President Zalman Schazar, Minister of Security Moshe Dayan, and General Chief-of-Staff David Eleazar.

112-113 A colorful kaleidoscope of day-to-day Israeli life.

114-115 In one of the narrow streets in Jerusalem, I came across this old watchmaker's shop.

116 A religious Jew has taken his child along to pray at the Wailing Wall.

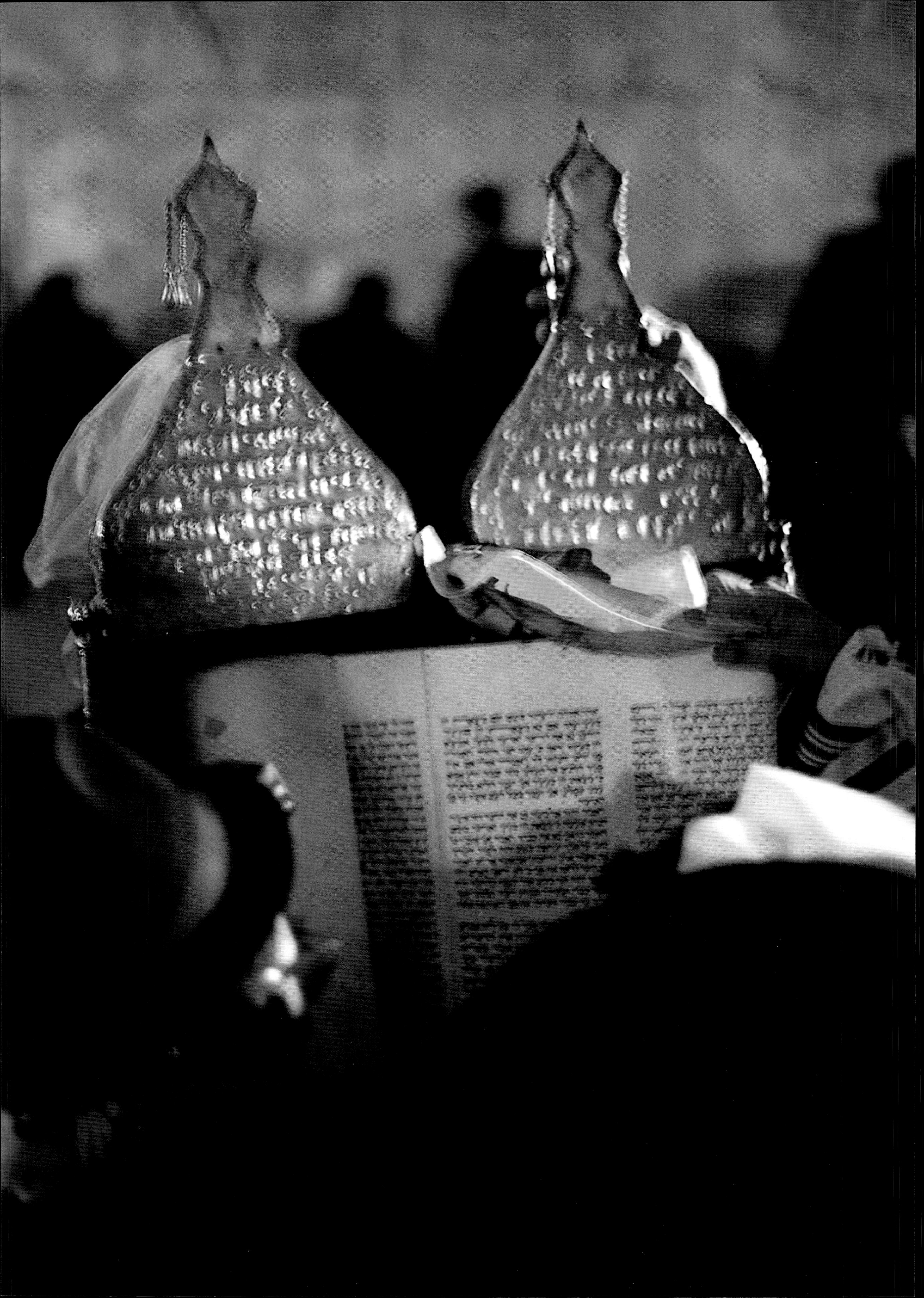

121 On October 6th, 1973, on one of the highest Jewish holidays, named Yom Kippur (Day of Atonement), Egypt and Syria simultaneously attack Israel at the Suez Canal and on the Golan Heights. Israel's greatest accomplishment in the first hours of the new war is undoubtedly the mobilization of its forces from 115,000 to 400,000 men. The secret can be explained quickly: the country is small, but possesses over 400,000 telephones. Backed up by constant radio announcements, in a short time every member of the reserves knows when and where he is to report. Thousands of private cars and buses bring them to their units within hours.

Yet in this war it becomes clear that the technological gap between Israel and its Arab enemies has become much smaller. Expecially the Russian-supplied SAM 2, SAM 3, and SAM 6 anti-aircraft rockets make it difficult for the Israelis to utilize their air superiority.

122-123 In Tel Aviv, an Israeli listens to news reports from the front from a tiny transistor radio, simultaneously searching for information on war events in the daily newspaper.

124-125 For Israel and for America, it is important that one of these Russian-made wonder rockets be captured undamaged. Only through this procedure is the success-

ful development of a defense system to be hoped for.
On the western bank of the Suez Canal, Israeli soldiers succeed with this plan.

126-127   On the Golan Heights, the Syrians resist bitterly. Israeli veterans of the Six Day War of 1967 are surprised by the fighting spirit and courage of their Syrian adversaries. But the losses of the Syrians are much greater; they are forced to retreat from their positions. The Israelis advance toward Damascus.

128-129   After the Israeli armored forces have succeeded in constructing a bridgehead on the western bank of the Suez Canal, more and more tank units press through onto

the other bank and finally surround the Third Egyptian Army. The city of Suez is reached.

130-131   Since the situation has turned to the Israelis' favor and a decision is imminent, bringing the two world powers, America and the Soviet Union, into a conflict situation, on October 22nd, 1973, a resolution is adopted by the United Nations Security Council calling for an immediate cessation of hostilities. The fighting ends only after 36 hours and results in the signing of a Six-Point Agreement between Israel and Egypt. Syria signs a troop disengagement agreement. On the front, United Nations soldiers police the observance of the cease-fire. In the heavily damaged city of Suez, Egyptians and Israelis stand some 15 yards apart, between them the U. N. sentry.

132-133
134-135 The greatest worry of the Israeli government is the soldiers who have been taken prisoner, as well as the wounded. Mourning for the unusually high loss of lives stuns the population. The wounded are invited to attend a concert and folkloristic presentation in Tel Aviv, to give them some variety and distraction.

136-137 The joy of this young girl at the healthy return of her boy-friend from the Golan Heights battle front is reflected in her eyes.

138-139 Devastated village in the battle area of the Golan Heights.

140-141 Remembrances for the dead at Rachel's Tomb on the edge of the city of Bethlehem.

142-143
144 In the first week of November, a great memorial service takes place at the Wailing Wall in Jerusalem. Thousands of men and women and young people remember the dead of this war which has been fought with the most modern weapons, which tore deep gaps in the ranks of able-bodied Israelis. Everywhere mourning, grief, lamentations.

149   Christmas in Bethlehem.
For Christmas Eve, many
thousands of believers from
all parts of the world stream
to the birthplace of Jesus
Christ.

150-151   The Church of the Nativity in
Bethlehem and the Church
of the Holy Sepulchre in
Jerusalem have been holy
sites for Christians for
centuries. Since the early
Christian era, a grotto here
has been considered the
birthplace of Jesus. The first
basilica was built by
Constantine the Great in
325 A. D. Today the foun-
dations of the earliest Church
of the Nativity can still be
seen, despite the many
changes and additions. The
Church of the Holy Sepulchre

arches not only over the
grave of Jesus Christ, but
also over Golgotha, the
place where Jesus had to
suffer death on the cross.
In the Church of the Holy
Sepulchre, six religious
communities are represented
at present: the Roman
Catholics ('Latins'), the Greek
Orthodox, Armenian Ortho-
dox, Syrian Orthodox,
Coptic Orthodox, and the
Abyssinians.

152-153   In addition to the many holy
sites of Judaism and Christianity, Jerusalem also houses
important Islamic religious
sites. One of the most
significant is the Dome of the
Rock. The very harmonic
construction is decorated
with marble on the bottom

and with Persian faience on top. The powerful cupola is visible from all sides of Jerusalem. It is one of the most striking sights of the city. In the foreground, the bell tower of the Russian monastery.

154-155 In the so-called 'Catholicon,' one of the parts of the Church of the Holy Sepulchre reserved to the Greek Orthodox, religious members gather to hear the sermon.

156-157 Golda Meir handing over her ballot at a Jerusalem polling-place. New Year's eve, 1973-74, I wait several hours for her appearance before the international press. This great, courageous woman has sensed during the night as the votes are counted that, because of the unfavorable outcome of the war, major political changes are developing. Time works against her; disappointed, she resigns her office as Prime Minister.

158-159 The day on which, at sunset, the last candle in the menorah will be lit in celebration of Chanukah, I pay a visit to the soldiers in the dug-outs on the Golan Heights and to a kibbutz. Chanukah, the Festival of Lights (in November or December) celebrates the victory of Judas Maccabeus over the Syrians and commemorates the re-kindling of the temple lamps. Particularly during this holiday the close

connection between family
and religion is evident.

160-161 The winter sun is enough to
draw this old man outside
to sit in front of his house
and read, enjoying the
warming rays of the sun.

162-163 Everywhere in the country
one sees fields covered with
plastic foil, under which fruits
are grown. Through this
method, several harvests per
year can be achieved,
and damage by strong
changes in weather are
diminished.

164-165 The Israeli farmer has no
time to ponder over the
outcome of the war. The
earth must be prepared
for the new seed. Nature's

rhythm allows for no inter-
ruptions.

166-167 The sea is calm.
An angler tries his luck.

168-169 The war is forced from the
mind. On a family outing,
parents and children crowd
together for a group photo
on a destroyed tank.
Forgotten are the battles, the
explosions, the wounded
and the dead. Life, day-to-
day life, is stronger than the
past.

170-171 Happy, free from fear and
skepticism, these Israeli
children, the hope for the
future of this land, look at us.

172 Many months have gone by
since the cease-fire at the

Suez Canal and on the Golan
Heights. American Secretary
of State Kissinger travels
repeatedly to Cairo, Tel Aviv,
Beirut, and Damascus. Progress toward a lasting,
peaceful settlement of the
conflicts in the Middle East
has been minimal. Even the
United Nations in New York
has been unable to find
a solution. Much water will
flow by the banks of the
Jordan before Israel and its
neighbors are able to alter
the present situation and –
one hopes – learn to live as
neighbors, in peace.